Friendship

THE JOURNEY

Janice A. Euell

Friendship - The Journey
Copyright © 2021 by Janice A. Euell

Poetry

Library of Congress Control Number: *2021918628*
ISBN-13:   *Paperback:*   *978-1-64749-584-8*
            ePub: *978-1-64749-585-5*

Although every precaution has been taken to verify the accuracy of the information contained herein, the author and publisher assume no responsibility for any errors or omissions. No liability is assumed for damages that may result from the use of information contained within.

Printed in the United States of America

GoToPublish LLC
1-888-337-1724
www.gotopublish.com
info@gotopublish.com

Contents

Friendship
THE JOURNEY

This collection of poems is **my journey**. Called Friend Ship because of how important being a good friend really is, but that we take for grtanted. It is an honor to have a friend and a pleasure to be one to someone who can appreciate the value of your time and presence.

Janice A. Crowder Euell published her first collection of poetry in 2002, entitled Poetry in the key of Life. She was recognized by the INTERNATIONAL LIBRARY OF POETS CONVENTION in Washington, DC as one of the POETS OF THE YEAR 2002. She recited her poem entitled 'I Thought of You today.' Dedicated to her late husband, Raymond P. Euell, who left too early the year before.

Prior to publishing her first collection, her poems have been featured internationally in other publications.

» Her poem, *"With Love"* published in the year 1999 in the International Library of Poetry's *"Visions of Beauty"* Collection,

» Her poem *"That's When I Cry"* was published in the year 2000 in the International Library of Poetry's *"Eternal Songs"* Collection,

» *"Love Without Happiness"* published in the year 2000 in the International Library of Poetry's *"The Road That Never Ends"* Collection

In 2011, another book signing was held celebrating her second book entitled *"Friend... Ship,* "in Capital Heights, Maryland. The collection continues to receive 5-star ratings after 10 years and is still available on Amazon and Barnes and Noble sites.

And now, you are invited to join her on the next leg of her journey in poetry as she proudly presents

'Friendship-The Journey."

Dedicated to my family and friends, whose positive energy puts the wind in my sails.

Friend Ship

Called so because some friends
Pass like ships in the night
Here today and gone tonight.
Friend ship because everyone
On board is familiar
Consoling and close, real
close?
Must be a good thing to have
A friendship as we struggle
To call each other friend
Friendship because of the heavy
Load that being a friend actually is.
Took much is taken for granted
As a friend.
To be a friend is not to be a pest
A reporter, always inquiring
Being there does not mean
Every day in the way.
Friend and ship were joined together
To support each other - when needed
To console as required
To meet when desired.
Friendship a vessel to be loved and admired.

Janice A. Euell

The Beast Within

Humans perceive themselves as heads above everything.
Men especially think their intelligence makes them superior
But to their females, they spend little time understanding her.
Women spend useless hours wanting to tame men
And then they get trampled trying to calm the beast within.

Men wake up! Know that the skin you're in is simply a disguise
because you're more like the wild kingdom that you realize
Oh yeah, you're a lion, lazy and sleeping on the ground
Waiting for the lioness to share the food she found.
A hyena's ravenous appetite is like yours, it'll eat anything
Nothing is too distasteful to be harnessed by the beast
within.

Like a snake sliding cautiously across the jungle floor
You have women who love your rattle, but you always want more
Having children and leaving them to fend for themselves for life
Not caring if they got devoured as they struggle and fight.
The beast within drives you and causes a loud roar
But women need you to be someone they can
adore.

It's very difficult to challenge you and be your friend
Because you can't release the beast that's within.

The Warrior Without a War

Anger, rage, no regard for life, a frown
On your face cannot be washed around
From zero to sixty in a flash
Ready to pounce on anyone in your path
Yes, you are the warrior without a war.
No need to leave home and go abroad fighting the enemy
with weapons to destroy them
No need to suit up like your battalion
'cause your war is personal--- it's within
Turmoil, strife.

Janice A. Euell

Time

It's a time and place for everything
A time to dance, protest a time to sing
There's a time to stand up instead of against the wall
Better known for something than nothing at all
Time changes, it moves up and down and frustrating as that is,
it comes back around, we've time out, time being,
and time on the tick tock wasting time,
Time after time and a time clock
It's a lot about time that we just don't get
especially when time anagrammed is emit
Time decides who stays young and who gets old that's a fact
Time turns your smooth face into a road map.
We say we don't have time to do that or this.
Have a good time for the moment- don't worry what you miss
You can't save time; it doesn't collect any interest or dividend
When time runs through a sieve, look at the mess you're in
We say we don't have time but that's just not true
until times runs out, what else you gonna do
Don't let time take over and become your master
Because the end of time seems to come much
faster
Take your Time.

The s s s s s Snake

This animal has been living in the history since the beginning
Supposedly it was the cause of Eve and Adam sinning
It shimmies and shakes its tail to give you warning
Yet humans think they have the power to charm him
It doesn't knock on your door to interject its poison
Human presence in its domain just plainly annoys him
We track them down 'cause we want their venom
But we wouldn't need it if we'd just avoid them.
Snakes don't need our help to survive, don't forget
Their species has been here since day one, and haven't gone yet
When you tread into their space, their cunning and wit
You deserve the agony you'll feel when you get bit

Janice A. Euell

In The Jungle

Way out on the Serengeti cutting trees with a machete
Watching birds soar magically through the air
There's a cunning cougar in the bush, don't know where.
Tiger up in the tree licking his fur
Looking for his cub but can't find her
The agile cheetah can run so fast
Her incredible speed makes it hard to pass.
The mighty and majestic king of beast rules his pride
while the lioness provides the feast
These are the scenes that one can see---
In the midst of the jungle grows one acacia tree.

Bed of Music

Now I lay me down on a bed of music
Listening to my heart as each note flows through it
The thump of the drums echo in my ear, my desire
laying on my bed of music sets my soul on fire
Music touches in places you can't see
Soothing, caressing, massaging me
Like a masseur as a professional in his trade
This is no time for the music to fade
Music is an injection of rhythm that flows through the veins
It takes you to height s that you will not experience ever again
When you kick back on your bed of music each day
It cleans and replenishes your spirit in a special way
When you wake with music on your mind and put the notes to work
As you walk, those pains you had no longer hurt
Music heightens your awareness and covers you
Like standing under a waterfall or feeling the morning dew
You don't have to have the blues to love the message it has
As you don't have to be a musician to feel the pulsating flow of jazz
When you can understand where music begins and ends
How the notes come together in a spiritual blend
You will have found your bed of music, be still and absorb it
Grab your big soft pillow, turn up the volume and enjoy it.

Janice A. Euell

Don't Stop The Music

Don't stop the music 'cause if you do
You will see how much life has affected you
You love music whether jazz or the blues
Country and western, classical and opera too
Swaying with the beat of the mighty drum
Taping your feet waiting for that feeling to come
The harmonica crying out a soothing tune
The sound of the saxophone taking you to the moon
Ddon't stop the music keep it in your soul and inspire
Have life deliver resounding tones sounds that rekindle a fire
Don't stop the music use it, feel it and don't forget
That you've just started to live it

On a Cruise

Going on a cruise is a vacation you chose
You are on the water where the spirit of God flows
Flags waving in the tropical air
Bills back home but you don't have a care
Enjoy the wine, friends, and, ,song
You'll be back in the race before long
Swim, play game consume good exotic food
If you could stay there. you would
This is the kind of life everyone can use
Unique experience while you were on a cruise

Janice A. Euell

The Jazz Singer

Blues conjure up relationships gone bad,
hip hop gotcha rapping wrapping
Rhythm and blues get your feet tapping
Gospel music uplifts you and its words linger
But nothing touches your soul like a jazz singer
Bluegrass and country have lots of stories to tell
Opera appeals to some and others noy so well
Those oldies but goodies make you pat your feet
The jazz singer makes you move to a different
beat
Head nod to and fro as closed - reminiscent of memories long ago
For moments in time, you don't realize you are moving
Hard to be mean when the jazz singer scats
You start to wonder where they're at where there are where they're at
It's the freedom to imitate an instrument while listening to one
More powerful is the voice than listening to the saxophone
The piano like a bird with a melodic chirp
Just sit back and watch the drummer work
The jazz singer delivers a beat so intense
No rhyme or reason don't need to make sense
The blende od drums, piano, horns and vocal tones
Have you humming those beats on your way home.

The Songwriter

With a pencil or pen, your thoughts manifest
Goodness, sadness love songs ior success
So often you write about love and how it hurts
If love is so painful, what then is it worth
The songwriter writes of love like a curse or a hex
But if love is not about caring, is it all about sex?
Is falling something to do over an over again?
Songwriter it's frightening to hear your lyrics
Love - you might want to steer clear of it
Without love the songwriter would rather die
In love sounds more like committing suicide
You write of love, hurting and cheating
Not of the kind of love that keeps your jeart beating
The thin between love and hate, try to understand
Frankie and Johnny were lovers, he was her man.
For God so loved the world, he gave his son
Someone had to die before all was said and done
Songwriter this thing called love is too much to bear
So I think I will settle for someone to care.

Janice A. Euell

Chill

Just chill out
You would, but you don't know what it's all about
Just chilling, take a chill pill
Oh, how great it is to chill
Just chill so simple yet complicated
So many similarities
Moderate, but unpleasant coldness, so defined
Others use it to unwind.
Yeah no one relates it toto anything sensual
Bu repeating the feeling would be eventual
In a flash, that feeling is somewhat instantaneous, no warning
It goes as quickly as it came – no harm in
Yet you'd like to have it repeated, you're reeling,
One gets goose bumps, tingling feeling,
Shivering, quivering, complete emptiness in the heart
Something that is useless, doesn't play a part
It's temporary, for a moment you are still
How awesome would it be if you could repeat it at will

Coulda Been

Don't you hate yourself beginning to end
When you think about, what you could have been
You couldae been anything or anybody if you had tried
You might have lived forever if you hadn't died
But I realize I'm happy in my own skin
Stopped worrying about what could been
What I coulda been does not mean a lot
Because I am content with what I've got

Janice A. Euell

What Time is Tomorrow

Never put off 'til tomorrow what you can do today
Tomorrow will be another day
What else about can one say
Actually, what time is tomorrow anyway?
Yesterday. we know because that time was ago
Today, we're living it, and it doesn't go slow
Don't plan for tomorrow because it never shows it's face
Just leaves you with an emptiness that you can't replace
We think of tomorrow, rename it in a twelve-o-millisecond
At that time tomorrow comes yesterday and new today
We talk about tomorrow but in reality
It's a topic for discussion day you never see
So what time is tomorrow who knows who cares
Plan for your todays if you want to get somewhere

Looking Out of My Window

I can see the seasons change
all kinds of trees, can't call them by name
not only the seasons I see
but any kind weather is sunny, raining, or windy
looking out of my window, I see the children playing
running with their families, grandparents praying
that piece of glass in front of me is not really a pain
that it I called that again and again
happily, they go about their everyday lives with glee
and occasionally I see people looking through my window at me.

Janice A. Euell

Volcano

Extreme heat pulsating, rhythmic, turmoil boiling
Volcano
Waiting for the day they can be free
VOLCano
Bursting into the air telling finally
VOLcano
Like anger building, waiting anxious anticipated
Looking for the unexpected it is a the mountain with an upset stomach
Rumbling
TEMperature climbing
Slowly rising to the top eating inhaling and exhaling
It wants to get out, volcano erupting then falling
VOLCANOOOOO!!!
Erupteding!!!
Aaaaah!

Life is

a bag of marbles reds, greens and blues

clouds clear with all different hues

like a song with Gladys and one pip

like a boat struggling in the wind with one sail

like building a house with one nail
great happiness yet some sad
a lot of things wonderful and some bad.
a smorgasbord of lights and bows
timeless, enjoy the beauty of rainbows
despite all the unpredictability
Life Is

Janice A. Euell

In The Name Of Love

Cheating, lying, stealing, abuse, pain.
Crying and constant neglect
In the name of love., don't
understand it yet
Love is so wonderful indeed
Why don't we all get what we need
It's in psalms poetry and weather in the sky
We strive for love from man or God
and we can't understand things
Children crying, hunger and flood
This we all do in the name of love

Turn The Page

If your life is really an opened book
perhaps, you'd like to take another look
at the way life has come thus far
and size up what you want and who you are

When life comes full speed and hits you in the chest
like a raging bull, you can't deal with the rest
of the challenges, it leaves you in a daze
enough drama — now you want to turn the page

On the next page, you want to find
something that will give you peace of mind
if on the next page, it's more of the same sadness
then turn two pages to skip the madness.

The foreword of your life summarizes
your life so Succinctly, one realizes
that each page of your life should be happy not sad
your deeds should all be meaningful, not bad.

When one reaches climax, suspense building
you hope you've set a pattern that is fulfilling
Turn the pages 'til you reach the end
Where your enemy is now your best friend.

If you read the acknowledgments and you're not in it
no more pages to turn, find another book and begin it
if all the pages in your life haven't been accurately related
and the facts are not like you anticipated

Janice A. Euell

Turn The Page

If the passion, praise, you wanted is gone
then pick up a pen and write a book of your own.

The beginning?

You Can't Do That No More

Children playing in the street
warm rain running across your feet
playing tag in a swimming in a cool stream
memories that today seem more like a dream
getting penny candy from the corner store
you can't do that stuff no more.

Watching your neighbor's house when no one 's home
caring for children that were not your own
giving food and clothing to those in need
even though you have thirteen to feed
you just can't do that no more.

Find a good woman or a good man
make each other happy anyway you can
then with each passing hour
your good times and turn sour
you shouldn't do that no more.

Those lovely children that you used to love
now instead you ignore the value they could
have all your life
by replacing it with instead of lot of strife.
You don't have to do that no more.

Janice A. Euell

Just For A Minute:

Just for a second in a day
I want the world to turn my way
just for a minute I like to see
a crystal ball with my future in it.
In an hour, my wish is this
that I could spend a dime I wouldn't miss.
One day without confusion, chaos
in the world pretending to want
peace at all cost.
A year has gone by, it seemed infinite
despite the craziness,
I have enjoyed my life, if just for a minute.

Never Loved

Shame to say, proud to boast
Telling you, not seriously, that I love you the most
So many of them are for the wrong reasons
Taking abuse from others season after season
I never fell in love because falling brings pain
I never want to hide teardrops in the rain.

When a woman in love as good as it gets
Until you realize you do it all just for sex,
Sex you don't have to earn, just go home
To find that special someone and not be alone
The world might be better off if you never loved
Concentrate on having sex and let it be done.

Janice A. Euell

Until You Know Peace

You can't know
true satisfaction
judging other's reaction
you won't be able to find a true release
until you know peace.

Peace is a state of mind
doesn't matter if you're deaf, crazy, or blind
it's the feeling you have deep within
that's where true peace really begins.

A period of tranquility that says everything is all right
you can relax dream, night after night
except you feel that calmness also during the day
until you know peace you won't understand what I have to say.

In The Meantime

The future you must plan it tomorrow not here
yet mysterious things you can't understand
memories some to remember
others to forget
but in the meantime.

You're going to buy that new car,
invest in a luxurious house
I want to go to the movie,
it might be bizarre
you wish folks would just tell it like it is
but in the meantime. . .

Hopes, dreams, aspirations put on hold
because you're planning instead of doing
it doesn't wait till the reality of life turns cold
in the meantime, as you wait, you might just forget.

Janice A. Euell

Frustration

Too many medications to handle any situation
that brings complications resulting in sheer frustration
Noise levels too extreme makes you want to scream
nothing is as it seems
the sanity to be redeemed
Frustration over little things that grow in credibly big
seeing a huge tree when it's only a twig
frustration and being somewhere when you want to
be any place exotic feels so good before,
but you forget it.
complications
situation
frustration

I've Given You

I've given you the best that I can
talked to you in words you can understand
walked with you giving you courage and direction
loved you, lavishing you with affection
Now that I've given you the best I must give
this is the foundation for the life you must live
the courage you need the inspiration you crave
the strong roots I've given you will take you to your grave
No one will have the ability to strip your power
your endurance fortifies itself by the hour.
Fly with the confidence stay away from the ledge
I've given you all the tools to give you the edge

Janice A. Euell

What Made You That Way

Robbing, stealing killing you went astray
what made you that way
you need love, you don't care who
has winning love done so much damage to you

Living the life of a hermit staying inside
inadequacies, fear, loneliness you can't hide
something burning making you scared to be in society
going from room to room with your anxiety
what made you that way?
Believing more like grieving but you went on without delay
God made you that way.

Smiling

Smiles— reassuring, bright and cheerful
turned inside out into something fearful.
Even though you smile, you can't see it's a fact
it may be menacing or one you can't forget
The intent of the smile may put you at ease
a grin on your face so it depends on what you believe
is that smile of approval, something you crave
or is it a fake like the royal wave?
You're behind your smile so you can't see
what kind of expression you meant for me
your smile of acceptance might need to be amended
what I see, you may not have intended
You think you know, and you do to some degree
Those smiles relative to what you perceive.
So when you smile make sure that it's true
Because the world does not always smile with you.

Janice A. Euell

A Poem On Your Heart

There is a poem on your heart,
I feel something you want to say,
don't conceal it it's about someone you cherish,
you don't dare to tell the person how much you really care.

There is a poem on your heart, I see it l growing deep inside,
You can't believe it when a smile slips across your face
when you imagine all the romance and warmth you feel within
begin go ahead and write your feelings down
don't hesitate, tomorrow may not come around
saying things that someone wants to hear
you are only held back by your own fear

Write that poem that's on your heart today
how can those feelings be returned if you don't say
what's in your heart, you may lose the love design for you
all the lines don't have to rhyme, as long as they're true.

The Comedians

They arrive on the stage saying something funny
for that, they want us to pay them money
their s joke sometimes funny most times not
but we want to laugh, for a short period our woes forgot.
Or is this the time for a comedian to let laughter hide his tear
so the need to laugh even for a minute is for all of us here
is the comedian making us laugh with their contrived baner?
Or are we there cause we want to hear others' laughter?
Laughing instead of crying lasts for that moment
funny or not that's the way we all want it
laughter helps us cover up the wars, crimes, in the newspaper
women acting so badly, being bitchy, we must hate her.
The comedians help us focus on the junk we do
That is said in es but is many times true
Let laughter be the medicine you take to feel good
Cause the comedians sure hope you would.

Janice A. Euell

Idioms

There's a time and place for everything
It's not over 'til the fat lady sings
Can't judge a book by its cover
And the buck stops here

They can continue but doesn't continue mean that anyway.
Why all the ado about a phrase
When all you need is to just say it.
Our need to be so mysterious
Only makes more of us furious.
Filling sentences with useless refrain
Using those idioms that you must explain.
Having to tell what's meant by a phrase
Defeats its purpose, mad at the one that created it.
Omit the idioms say what you mean
Then you won't have to explain anything,
If you do that earnestly you'll see
Idioms should be eliminated from the dictionary.

Cocoon

Wrapped up in a world of confusion,
Waiting my time
My shelter from the world's transgression
Soon will be gone until the next cycle
Trapped in a self-made prison,
Praying to just be free.
Metamorphosis slowly taking place
New shape forming gradually
Nervously waiting to show the
World my new beauty
I am out on my own.

Janice A. Euell

I Want To Talk About Life

With a scholar,
Or with the village idiot
With a child
Or with a homeless guy
I want to talk about life,
Nothing could satisfy me more
Than to know what they think
About politics, about crime,
What would they change?
Anyone ever ask your opinion?
Or do things just happen
And you nod with unquestioning approval?
Don't you want to talk about life?
In every walk of life, there is a person
That has something profound to say,
But who really asks them anything?
We're too busy believing that we have the only answers

I want to talk about life
With a child just learning how to talk
What are their first words, their first sentence?
And what was it about?
Food, sleep, something to drink?
Life is much more than what
I think or what you think you know,
It's about a noun,
Persons, places or things,

Or, maybe I don't want to talk about life,
Maybe just living, loving, caring
About myself and my surroundings
Is enough to turn my nouns into adjectives.
Then, I can write about life.

Janice A. Euell

I Wrote A Poem

In the depth of my soul
Is a story n'er to be told.
I wrote a poem that no one will ever see
'cause it reveals a very private part of me
Under the laughter lies a sadness
That sometimes gets me down.
B'neath the smiles, a frown, that
Creeps into my being when no one is around
The rain that gently falls from the skies
Are mere droplets compared to the tears that fall from my eyes.
I wrote a poem praying that emptiness would
Not again visit me and hope to regain
That part of me that is still somewhat sane.
Putting my thoughts on paper
Is a whole lot safer than taking my pain to the street
And having a lifeless soul at my feet
So a poem is my salvation.

If I Could

if I could stay forever, would I?
or would I just prefer to die.
Living in a weakened condition,
Is not that a frightening premonition?
If a bird could no longer fly
Would it try?
Or remain on land and let life pass it by?
If I could fly, would I?
Being larger, do you yearn to be thin?
Or am I content in my own skin?
When my stature is small,
Why do I pine to be tall?
Does a bottle want to be a can?
A boy can't wait to be a man.
When your looks don't change even when you try
Can only be achieved if you're a butterfly.
Resentment to contentment? I can.

Janice A. Euell

If You Do Nothing

A flat tire in the morning.
Leaky faucet that didn't leak the night before.
Another ache, another pain,
All of these things happen,
If you do nothing.
If you do nothing but rise
A new problem will materialize,
If you mind your own business
Life brings you grief and
Complications arrive unsolicited at your door.
Power outages
Refrigerator won't freeze – it did the night before.
Washer stopped washing,
Dryer stopped drying,
And you did absolutely nothing to make things happen.
No need to create problems for yourself
They come freely and unprovoked.
They will rise and set,
The wind will blow, flowers will bloom,
If you do nothing.
Crime and violence remain on your street.
Politicians that don't consider your issues,
The wrong person gets in office.
The world does not become a better place,
If you do nothing at all.

In The Mornin'

Looking at my situation tonight, it looks pretty sad.
Whenever heard of any person's life being so bad?
Nothing going right, things comin' up without warning
But my mother told me,
"things always look better in the mornin'"

Well, mama, God love her, I've tried to believe
In her wisdom, and I've tried to achieve.
Workin' hard every day trying to do the right thing
Wanna get up in the morning' and hear the birds sing.
But life tonight is pretty much the same as yesterday
Getting up in the mornin' is just God's way
Of telling us to have faith, there's a new day dawnin'
And truthfully, with all my trials,
There's nothing like getting up in the mornin'.

Janice A. Euell

Looking At The Sky

Looking at the sky through the trees,
Your view is sometimes obstructed by the leaves
In the winter, you see the foliage disappear
Then the blue sky seems so beautiful and clear.
When the ice clings to the tree branches,
The sky may be grayer, but the ice enhances.
It's beauty its charm and grace
Looking at the sky even then brings a smile to my face.
The sky is constantly changing, different hues, shapes, and sizes.
The reds, oranges and blues and many other panoramic surprises.
Unlike the trees, the sky gives no indication ofseason
If gives us magnificence and light shows all year for no real reason.
Blue sky, white clouds, bright sunshine and clear.
Gray skies, dark clouds bring rain during the year
Violent weather could bring tornadoes and storms
But our clouds, delight, excite and forewarn.
Clouds help us predict the weather, at least we try,
You see, you can learn so much just looking at the sky.

Night

Hark! The night falls
Rainbows over the land disappear
Haunting eyes stare down from the sky
No color, everything is black or white
Lo' the mystery of the night.
The night casts shadows
Reflection of the soul
That hideth behind eyes of glistening coal
Cryin' out for salvation
In a story yet to be told.
The night is deceiving
Things unthreatening during the day
Take on different shapes in the night
Chillin' your inner psychic,
Making you believe things your eyes do no see.
Yet the night has its intrigue ability
Makes you see things in a different light
It presents more challenges.
The beauty of the day doth not reappear,
When you are no longer here.

Janice A. Euell

Sailing

Such a panoramic view
Blue sky, not a cloud
Waves gently massage
The rocky shore
The motion of the tide
Stretching out to touch land, then receding
Sails in different colors
Boats, all sizes
Yachts, speed boats
Ocean rising up and then exhaling
Relaxes your mind and spirit.
The water takes you to another special place.
Makes your soul feel relief to be
In unison with the elements
Sailing, riding the waves like a bronco.
When you're feeling this good
You want to float.
Now, all you need is a boat.

Seasons Of Rain

Winter, the rain comes, cold air turns it to ice.
Nothing you wear every seems to suffice,
When the cold winds blow, there's no doubt
That any sensible person will want to go out.
Flower buds peeking out in the morning dew
Opening their arms to welcome you
A light soft sprinkle starts life in the spring
Getting caught in the rain is a delightful thing.
Summer raindrops, warm and cool
A walk in the rain, no umbrella, just the winter and you.
Thunderstorms are raindrops gone made
Some of the worse we've ever had
Tornadoes, flooding, and hurricanes
So vicious they gave them all names.
The rhythm of the raindrops signal it's fall.
Pumpkins. The rain brings a great harvest for all.
The seasons of rain come and go no matter the season,
It can bring joy or pain for no obvious reasons.

Janice A. Euell

Soarin' Through The Clouds

Soarin' through the clouds
Many places I can see
Old and new, big and small
My spirit runs free.
I fly high on days when exhilaration I feel
And low at times when frustration is real.
In the clouds, soft
Fluffy ones, white and blue
Cleanse your soul
Your worries subdued.
A trip in the clouds high up above
Would not be possible without God's love.
Soar through the clouds with an open mind
Peace in the clouds you shall find.

Special Event

As a seed, I lay dormant inside
Waiting for my time to arrive.
At the mercy of someone else to decide.
Waiting patiently for the ultimate surprise
Of being able to open my eyes
And for the world to hear my cries.
No one knows what I must endure, it's not right
Being in limited space, wet with no light.
Angry, but can't put up a fight.
I struggle and struggle trying to get out.
No one knows what my unrest is about.
It's just contractions, no doubt.
To waiting hands, I am delivered.
To another prison, just bigger,
Special event. Heaven sent or hell bent.

Janice A. Euell

Stand Up And Be Counted

You, yes you, get off your lazy behind
Open a newspaper and see what you can find.
Turn on the radio and listen to the news
Call them up and give them your views.
Get the remote and turn the television on to see
If there's a situation brewing in the Middle East.
It's time for you to stop letting everyone else do things for you.
Check out what's happening and see what you can do.
Stand up and be counted, be proud and active
Find a situation in which you can be proactive
Many lives were lost for you to have certain rights
For some things, you must take a stand and fight.
But fighting each other is not one of the choices
There are other ways for others to hear our voices
Stand up and be counted, exercise your right to vote
If you're not paying attention, you may miss the boat.
Teach your children to care about the land,
When you see a child in despair, lend a helping hand.
If you don't take a position on what's right and wrong,
You'll continue to complain, singing that same old song.
Your participation is solicited and appreciated, indeed,
To make decisions about our country's many needs.
So stand up and be counted or be seated and settle for less
Until you become a part of the solution, you really can't
Expect the best.

The Day the Skies Cried

The pain of waking, without you.
Heart aching
Sadness,
Tears in my eyes
Was the day the skies cried.
The unfilled desires
Hurt from a love gone bad
The love of your life died
On that day, the skies cried.
Heartbreak, love forever gone
Been here and now you're alone
The rains come to hide the tears
That fall from your eyes
Every time the skies cry.

Janice A. Euell

That's When I Cry

When love is lost and can't be found
Children are hurting, no parents around,
A beggar with no food to eat
A lonely soul with no shoes on his feet,
That's when I cry.
Hearing the wind howling on a cold winter night
Or a baby crying in its room from fright,
A mama whose child lost his life to crime
A father searching for a child he can't find,
That's when I cry.
When war turns our neighborhoods into debris
Refugees fighting 'cause they want to be free
Tornadoes destroying everything in their way
Floods and hurricanes, the devastation, the decay,
That's when I cry.
A rose delivered because someone really loves me
Thoughtful notes, kind gestures, a heart full of glee,
Friends, family, bring flowers while you are alive
Waiting arms to caress me as I arrive,
That's also when I cry.

The Noise

My inner spirit is quiet.
I hear the thoughts in my mind.
Thoughts about living
Those regrets about dying
I pray for the noise
With the noise I put
Unpleasantries to rest.
I don't have to listen to my inner pain.
I bring in the noise but
Tribulations come again.
Horrible things I did, deceit, lies
Neglect and crimes
Though I'm not trying, sad memories
Take over my inner being.
I hear my noise but for you, it takes a new slant
You want to forget life's miseries, but you can't
Some things in your past you want to avoid
By keeping the volume turned up on the noise.

Janice A. Euell

They Will Come To Your Funeral

It's sorta odd and somewhat strange

Many people know your name,

Your friend they claim to be
Your face they seldom see,
But they will come to your funeral.
A card, some flowers while you live
None of these will they give.
Kind words, a gift, a shoulder on which to cry,
Fail to show they love you until you die.
Sadness, problems, disappointments, deeply blue,
No one to listen or care about you.
Sit alone and ponder, wonder why
Friends don't like you til you expire.
And, they will come to your funeral.
They wouldn't come to visit not for a minute.
Is the world a better place without you in it?
Are they crying at your funeral because you're gone?
Or sad 'cause it took you so long?
No mat'r, they will come to your funeral.

When Do You Stop?

Violence, hatred, and many lives wasted
All because of you
'cause you can't face it
What are going to do?
When do you stop being the game
Being pursued by the hunters
Drug users and dealers know the hunters by name
And they'll know your name when you go under.
Crime and chaos have become a part of your life
For more than twenty years
You've abandoned your children and your wife
Leaving them at home in tears.
A job to you is a foreign, unimaginable thing
An enigma if you will
You never gave your wife a wedding ring
You know all of this and still......
You don't stop. You've outta control
Your life is a terrible mess
Can't help you, but save your child's soul
Start anew – just confess.
'cause if you can't stop
Life passes you by
Just when you decide to stop
May be your time to die.

Janice A. Euell

Why Is It?

That the other line always seems to move faster?

Or the grass on the other side always looks greener?
Why do some lives end in disaster?
And no matter how nice you are, the meaner
Just keep getting meaner.
That you love someone, and they love someone other than you?
That one foot is bigger than the other?
Can't seem to find a friend that is true.
An act of kindness doesn't come from a sister or brother?
Sometimes you wonder, indeed you do.
Why the stars hang precariously in the sky.
Why people think there's a man in the moon? That's not true.
Sometimes the wondering makes me want to cry.
I ask myself why is it? And no answer comes right away.
I ask others and they must speculate.
Instead of continuing to ask why, I put my queries aside,
Or just plain disregard it, 'cause the answers really can wait.

Why Must I Be The Glue?

Why must I be the glue that holds everything together
Consoling everyone until their lives get better?
When tears fall from their faces like rain.
When their faces are gently contorted from pain.
When things go wrong and they don't know what to do,
I hear the call, dear Lord, to provide the glue.
Why must I be the glue that binds a family in love?
In this a gift of compassion, an inspiration from above?
When a child somewhere cries in pain from abuse.
Must be the times I want to sleep, but there's no use.
The empathetic side of me feels the pain and sorrow,
Of those long forgotten with no hopes for tomorrow.
When I see someone hungry with nothing to eat.
Or a person walking without shoes on their feet.
I feel drawn to find a way for their lives to renew
There I go again, Lord, wanting to be the glue.

God has apparently seen fit to bestow on me this
Precious gift.
To provide hope for those needing an inspirational lift.
Who am I to question or otherwise complain about what
I must do?
I guess, dear Lord, the answer is because you want me to.

Janice A. Euell

You Don't Know Me

We have never been further apart.
Though I've wanted to be closer with all my heart.
I call but you're too busy or slow to react.
For some reason, you just can't call back,
Our lives have been intertwined for many years.
Yet you know nothing of my pleasures or fears,
When asked if I prefer a movie or a play
You wouldn't have much to say,
Because you really don't know me.
Strangers in your life about whom you know more.
I may be the stranger as I walk through your door.
My likes, favorites, or my whimsical toy
You don't know what things bring me joy.
Do I like to travel, or prefer to stay at home?
Is fear a factor when I'm alone?
Am I handling my afflictions well?
There's no way for you to tell
Why? Because you don't know me.

I Am An Artist

I am an artist with an inherent ability
To paint what I do or do not see.
The color of the sky can be what I want it to be
I can illustrate the calmness of an ocean or sea.

A person's face can be happy, sad or full of dismay.
A day can be cloudy with everything else gray.
From my palette I can create exactly what I feel.
A scene can be fantasy, or it can be real.
I can paint diplomats or a clown just joking,
But I can't paint anything when my heart is broken.
I can create a vision for all to see,
But I can't paint a love that lasts for eternity.
I can put on canvas my innermost thoughts and desires,
Which could be cold as the north or as passionate as fire.
I admire scenes and places of beauty, so I work my hardest
Using my palette to turn reality to dreams because I am

An artist.

Janice A. Euell

Piano Blues

Since I was a little girl, I loved the piano,

Where I got that feeling, I really don't know

My mama didn't play, neither did my Dad,

But play the piano is the fondest dream I ever had.

Those pearly whites and blacks look so intimidating,

Trying to decipher which key plays what tune - so frustrating!

I'm gonna sit on that bench put my fingers in place,

No F key or clef is gonna put a frown on my face.

Admittedly, my heart's racing, my hands shaking a bit,

No more nervous about that first note could I get.

It takes the left and the right sides of my brain,

To play an intelligible tune that you can call by name.

I practice until my fingertips turned blue,

And twinkle, twinkle little star was the best I could do.

So, I sat on that bench, posture upright.

Fingers in place, but I was still so uptight.

I'll conquer my piano blues by just whistling a tune.

And promise to get back to the ivory very soon

When perspiration no longer hangs from my brow,

I'll learn to play someday, but not now

Sexy Saxophone

Sassy notes, so soothing
Suddenly you feel like moving
Rocking gently from side to side
Emotions surfacing. You can't hide
That's the rhythm of the sexy saxophone.
It's perfect body. Such pizzazz.
Falling prey to the smooth jazz,
That emanates from its soul
Resulting in a sound so bold.
A romantic interlude.
The sound takes you to a new place
The look of contentment spreads over your face
Doesn't matter if it's music or song
Nothing can really go wrong
When you listen to the melodies from the saxophone
Sadness, problems all disappear
When sex sounds are all you hear.
Pleasure. Listening in a crowd or alone.
Nothing matches the soul stirring saxophone.

Janice A. Euell

The Painter

The Painter needed a world with a lot of color in it
His list of ideas for beauty seem infinite.
He looked at the sky and decided just blue would not do
So he chose a variety of colors and hues.
"Trees, what shall I do with them?" he said.
"Perhaps, a selection of green, yellow, brown and red."
"But, wait," He said, "something is missing to me.
I shall also paint rivers, oceans, and seas.
Everything seemed too flat for the world to be right
He needed majestic mountains rising to new heights,
To complete His idea of the perfect painting. He cried,
"There must be people here to see this and admire.
He stood and looked at this wondrous thing He had done
This perfect painting could not be duplicated by anyone
It was a masterpiece no other copies to be made
Everlasting beauty created that will never ever fade.
When He painted the day, He painted the night
But still something wasn't exactly right.
The day was full of beauty to appease the eye,
Which all disappeared when the evening drew nigh.
He decorated the night sky with stars and the moon
To light our way
Until we open our eyes to the dawn of a new day
Thanks to the Painter for creating such beauty
To protect it and take of it is now our duty.

A Mother's Love

Like a flower waking with the morning dew
Basking in the warmth of the sun, its spirit to renew
Like watching on a clear night, the stars above
Nothing surpasses the tenderness of a mother's love
Chastising you, she has your best interest at heart
She wants life's treasures for you from the start.
Asking you to do your chores, she's training
Telling you to wear rain gear when it's raining.
She is the doctor wanting your body and mind to heal
From any stress or strain you might feel.
As a psychiatrist, she listens intently to your woes
Like a general, she strategizes how to defeat your foes.
In a carpool, she is the driver to your track and field meet
As a chef, she prepares scrumptious meals for you to eat.
Her compassion and devotion run deep like still water
Making no difference between her son and daughter.

When you're down, she's there to cushion your fall
She's always available whenever you call.
She brings happiness and peace to your life like a dove
Nothing equals the depth of a mother's love.

Janice A. Euell

Happy Anniversary

With this ring, I thee wed,
On our wedding day is what we said.
Sacrifice and compromise all of our lives
Having children with an unpredictable wife.
Ove the years we have struggled to make ends meet
But through it all, we overcame every defeat.
In our years together, we have had great and bad times
Yet, you're the best husband I could ever find.
We have laughed together and yes, we have cried
We have lived through the truth and yes a few lies.
No matter what the consequence, we have survived
'cause we have love and compassion in our lives
Some say you deserve a medal and maybe you do
To live with me so long and perhaps that's true.
You helped me walk when I only thought I could crawl
And you've always been there to break my fall.
For this occasion, I must tell you what I feel, and I truly mean it
To have, to hold, is our fate for all eternity.

I Had A Need

I felt for the pillow
Where you laid your head,
My mind played the words
That you once said,
I had a need this mornin'
And I didn't know what to do.
The pain of your leaving
Was still fresh in my heart
I never dreamed that
Someday we'd part.
You left an emptiness in
A deep, dark place.
Tho' you're gone, every
Minute I see you face.
Where you've gone you
Will never return
Leaving my heart to fore'er yearn
For the love we once had
My spirit will never heal because your
Leaving has hurt me so bad.
I had a need that only your touch could fulfill
Many have tried, but no one ever will
I had a need this mornin' and I didn't know what to do
'cause I can't walk, touch or feel without you.

Janice A. Euell

Mother

She was mysterious,
Unpredictable, fun
And a little crazy.
A lady of leisure,
Confident and carefree.
Special because she
Gave birth to me.
Caring, forgivin', calculating.
Decisive and demanding
An accomplished chef, you'd
Love anything, she had her hand in.
In her, no comparison,
There will never,
Be another
Certain mysteries about her unraveled
As I became a mother.

You Were There

When I took my first breath
Took my first step.
As I started my first grade
The mistakes I made.
You were there when I had my first fight
I tried to run away with all my might.
A big step in my life
When I got a now wife.
When I had my first child
You greeted him with an adoring smile.
And my second blessed event
A girl who was also heaven sent.
You were there when losses in my life lead to despair
I was there when gray replaced the black in your hair.
For every special and blessed event, Dad,
you've been
A friend so true.
And now, it's my chance to be there for you.

Janice A. Euell

Your Legacies Live On

It is in your memory
That these lines are written
Neither of you we can think about forgetting
Your sons and daughters will thrive in love
Knowing that you rest peacefully above
In your light, our accomplishments shine
Your guidance and leadership were so divine.
We are happy that you were there when we were born
Because of you, your legacies live on.
All that we are or ever hope to be
Was because you set our minds free.
When we look at each other, your faces we see
We love and praise you as your legacies live on for eternity.
You were here but now you are gone from our sight
But your legacies live on, we try to do what's right.
Dedicated to the memory of my parents
Bessie Swinnie Crowder
William Martin Crowder

Hot Flashes

Hot flashes have a very bad reputation
Is there any truth in it,
You're okay now but
In just one minute
Sweating
Running for the door
Opening the windows.
Keep a handkerchief in hand,
Not thinking about a man,
Trying to cool and feel cool.
Instead, you look more like a fool.
People in heavy coats, buttoned to the neck
You're the only one sweating
Whole body soaking wet.
This had to be a punishment
Manufactured by Satan
No one else could conjour
Up such a hellish situation

How to identify a person with those hot flashes?
While you are standing still, they're the
Ones running fast past you
Not necessarily doing it with flair
Just rushing to the window to get some fresh air.

Janice A. Euell

Just Chillin'

Sipping tea, swinging in the breeze
Just watching the wind gently caress the oak tree leaves
Got a job to do, but sure ain't willin'
'Cause I'm much happier when I'm just chillin'
Bring on the lemonade while I'm rocking
Don't want to hear no one knocking
Ice cold drink to massage my mind
This is the best life a lazy mind can find.
Don't want no problems, no family or friends
Who can't understand the state of mind I'm in
When I'm chillin', I reject the noise
Made by men, women, little girls or boys.
Just me. Laid back, care and worry free
No problems bother me
If you can't imagine just how I'm feelin'
Then you need to find out what it feels like to be just chillin'.

My Tribulations

My back is aching so is my knee
The bottoms of my feet are as sore as can be.
I've walked a mile in shoes that are two sizes too small
Must have lost my mind shopping for them at the mall.
My eyes are blurred, sometimes can't see a lick
When darkness comes, glasses too thick.
My throat is dry, my back is starting to itch
I'm catching a cold, getting old, I don't know which.
You told me something yesterday, now I can't recall
Was it important? Don't know. Can't tell you at all.
My tribulations aren't as paramount as they seem.
'Cause I work up this morning and it was all a dream.

Janice A. Euell

Why Women Have Headaches

They live with
Make love to them
Fight over trivia
With Men
Because men can't find their socks
Lose their keys
Can't remember to get a loaf of broad
From the corner store
On their way home.
No, women don't know
What you want to eat.
Have to live with you and your
Smelly feet
And because you snore.
Women have headaches
because You won't ask for directions
Can't remember birthdays
Anniversaries and you
Don't know your children's first names.
A man's "where is my" syndrome
Can't find a thing in your own home.
What you're looking for is right in your face
One would think you rented the place
Your skull is looking for a tenant.
Nevertheless, God loves you
And
So do women!

Change Of Life

You got a bad attitude
You're rude
And loud.
Grow up make a new life for yourself now
Do you know how?
Make success a vow.
Stop blaming others for your sad mistakes
All that crying is a serious fake
Change your life before it's too late.
Realize you can do anything if you try
Make an effort.
Questioning you seems like you're on trial
No, it's just to get you out of self-denial
Set goals, achieve, experience life for a while.
This is your change of life request for you to do your best
Don't settle for less.
Changing your life is your destiny
Change it for you and not for me.

Janice A. Euell

Dark Cloud

There's a dark cloud hanging over your head
You should be happy but you're sad instead
There's a dark cloud hanging over your head.

There's a strange cloud enveloping your head

Change your life before you end up dead.
There is no future in death.
A dark cloud has you constantly and fearfully on the run
Miserable, when you should be having fun
That's a sad situation, ain't it?
The dark cloud won't leave you alone.
Childhood sadness and now you're grown.
Ain't it time to live now?
You lurk in the alley day by day like a rat
Robbing, stealing, set back after set back.
This is not a bad life, jut live it.
That dark cloud can be removed and it's not hard.
You just need to get a little closer to God.
Turn the black cloud into one with silver thing.

Without God you can do nothing, positive that is
Look for faith and happiness life gives
Fully appreciate this precious gift.
Yeah, lift that black cloud and bring yourself joy
Contentment and peace in life you can enjoy
The choice is yours
That dark cloud hovering up above
Can be changed with just a little love.
Love is not painful

I Can Say Yes

I can say yes because I am strong
Because I know what's right or wrong
Peer pressure they claim can destroy me
My parents taught me to love myself, how can that be?
I can't believe the hype I hear on the street
I'm told to dance to a different beat.
I can yes when there's a positive situation
To avoid possible incarceration.
Behind bars, I can't plan or dream
Isolation is as tough as it seems
I don't listen to you, what do you know?
You're burning your brains out on that stuff called blow.
I can say yes to a life without crime
Because the name on success is mine.

Janice A. Euell

It's You

I am a very special person with very special needs
I require the best, and certainly want to succeed.
I have an inspiration that's tried and true
And that inspiration, I believe, it's you.
It's you, I'm certain, you are always around
To listen when my heart is on the rebound.
When getting up in the morning is a chore for me
It's the memory of your smile that sets my soul free.
Yes, it's true, it's really you
Who lights the embers of my being
Who looks beyond what others are seeing
I am a happy person, full of excitement and glee
Concentrating on those things that satisfy me.
I'm wild, kinda silly and sometimes crazy
And yeah, I'm interesting, intriguing, and lazy.
But when I'm my best and everything else is tried and true.
I attribute my happiness to me and to you.

The Power Of One

It's really amazing what can be done
In life these days by the power of one.
Seeing litter on the street is tough
When you see a piece of trash, pick it up.
If one person agrees to be racially aware
No prejudice or animosity would be in the air.
As a volunteer, you can accomplish a lot
When you realize all the talent you've got.
If we care about the earth, appreciate fresh air
Each person must be prepared to do their share.
Don't point your finger accusingly at the other guy
You are the one who must tell your children why.
You neglected the earth and everything in it
You smoked and drank not remembering any of it.
Careless and confused, you've hurt everyone in your path
Just how long do you think this destruction can last?
Sure, you're just one person but so is everyone
It's exhilarating the difference we make as the power of one.

Janice A. Euell

Wings

On the wings of dissension
Are situations too critical to mention.
The wings of desperation and despair
Are laden with those who just don't care.
Outstretched arms give the appearance of wings
But illusions are very disconcerting things.
Wings are for soaring high up above
White clouds, majestic mountains, expressions of love.
With wings you could fly from fantasy to reality
Visiting every place in the world you've wanted to see.
Clipped wings injured one day in a storm and
Making you land bound for a while without warning.
To learn to survive on land when your domain is the sky
Makes life seem unfair and you wonder why.
Imagine your wings unfolded for flight
Taking you to new places soaring to new heights.
Imagine your ambition and goals as your wings
You will be able to accomplish some incredible things.

Chippin' Away At My Love

Broken promises
Blatant lies
Inconsistent behavior
Betrayal
You have started to chip away at my love.
Love started true.
Passionate, trusting, caring
Two hearts merged into one.
Years pass
Love taken for granted
It takes my love down another peg
Because you didn't do something you said
I loved you when our love was forbidden
When we had to keep our love hidden
I sacrificed some things quite personal
To have your love but worst of all
The fantasy faded; feelings started to erode.
Romantically, we are not where we used to be
Because you have destroyed that faith you see
Ev'ry lie, or act of deceit brings wrath from below
Because you have chipped away at my love
And shaped it into an unrecognizable emotion.

Janice A. Euell

In Your Eyes

Beauty, reflection, confidence, surprise
All this I see in your eyes.
Mystery, suspense, intrigue
Deep down it lies
In the area, the crevices behind your eyes.
Love, admiration, sadness, and grief
Tear falling from your eyes
Bring some relief
From the pain you feel deep inside
That you can't hide because of your eyes.
In your eyes, all emotions abide
No matter how hard you try to hide
Behind the blindfolds or dark sunglasses
The eyes watch carefully as your life passes.
Happiness, contentment, full of life and glee
A gleam in your eyes for the world to see
Broken promises you did not realize
Can't always be detected in your eyes.

My Best Friend

Who is that person so honorable and great?
So trustworthy and dependable and never late?
The one who always stands by me in thick or thin.
Who rescues me no matter what situation I'm in?
My best friend
My personal issues are discussed with the utmost care
When I am happy or sad, you're always there.
It doesn't matter to you if I'm on the bottom or the top
If I try a new project, you don't care if it's a flop.
You're my best friend
A peculiar person like me needs a person like you
Though we don't say l love you every day, we know it's true
On the road to adventure you're the best driver
During a nature hike you're always the survivor.
Since I met you, I've stop searching for a confidant
Because you're the person that I surely want
To share my good times or when my heart s on the mend
I can find no other person on whom I can depend.
I guess that's why you're my best friend.

Janice A. Euell

With Love

I think of the rain
Tapping gently on my windowpane.
I'm reminded how special you make me feel
And how comforting it is to know your love is real.
I smile because of how good I feel inside
And when I can't be with your sometimes, how I've cried
You mean so much to me, as I have told you
Many times, before,
But when I thought of you today, I wanted to tell you once more.
I love you and you are a special part of me
Because when I think of you, it makes me more than happy
I think of how crazy and silly you sometimes are
And how I am comforted to know that you're never far.
In other words, what I am trying to say
Is that you have impacted my life in a satisfying way.
I hope our relationship will endure all tests of time
Finding me in your arms and you in mine.
I love you

You Thought Of Me Today

When you thought of me today
What did you say?
How did you feel?
Was it surreal?
You thought of me today, didn't you?
I smiled when your call came through
My heart pounded hearing your voice
Gratified that you've made me your choice.
Loving someone like I love you this minute
Makes this a wonderful life with you in it.
I'll think of you until the end of time
I was in your thoughts today and you in mine.
When you thought of me today
Could you wait until the end of the day?
To caress, to hold, to be close to me again.
It's so comforting to have you as my friend.

Janice A. Euell